SUPERCARS

MERCEDES-BENZ

Christine Webster

AV2
www.openlightbox.com

Step 1
Go to **www.openlightbox.com**

Step 2
Enter this unique code
BALKTO5RI

Step 3
Explore your interactive eBook!

AV2 is optimized for use on any device

Your interactive eBook comes with...

Contents
Browse a live contents page to easily navigate through resources

Audio
Listen to sections of the book read aloud

Videos
Watch informative video clips

Weblinks
Gain additional information for research

Slideshows
View images and captions

Try This!
Complete activities and hands-on experiments

Key Words
Study vocabulary, and complete a matching word activity

Quizzes
Test your knowledge

Share
Share titles within your Learning Management System (LMS) or Library Circulation System

Citation
Create bibliographical references following the Chicago Manual of Style

This title is part of our AV2 digital subscription

1-Year K–5 Subscription
ISBN 978-1-7911-3320-7

Access hundreds of AV2 titles with our digital subscription.
Sign up for a FREE trial at **www.openlightbox.com/trial**

SUPERCARS

MERCEDES-BENZ

CONTENTS

MERCED

ES-BENZ

MERCEDES-BENZ SUPERCARS

Great care goes into making supercars. These cars are fast and expensive. They are also **luxurious** and **exclusive**. Companies only make a limited number of them every year.

Mercedes-Benz is renowned for its innovative technologies and stunning designs. Drivers around the world enjoy the power and elegance of Mercedes-Benz vehicles. The company makes luxury passenger cars, sports cars, and supercars.

Mercedes-Benz plans to make only **275 Mercedes-AMG One** cars.

About **2.1 million Mercedes-Benz** passenger cars were sold in 2020.

CARL BENZ AND GOTTLIEB DAIMLER

German **engineers** Carl Benz and Gottlieb Daimler came to great technological advances around the same time. In 1886, Carl Benz **patented** a vehicle powered by a gasoline engine. That same year, Daimler and Wilhelm Maybach, another engineer, built a different gasoline-powered, four-wheel vehicle. They did so by adding an engine to a **stagecoach**.

Both Benz and Daimler owned successful companies. These companies changed names and structures over the years. Finally, in 1926, the two companies **merged** to form Daimler-Benz AG. The first cars under the Mercedes-Benz brand arrived on the market that year.

Bertha Benz, Carl Benz's wife, had an important role in the creation of her husband's first vehicle. She financed its development and was the first person to drive it on a long distance.

MAP OF GERMANY

The Mercedes-Benz Headquarters and the Mercedes-Benz Museum are in Stuttgart. Mercedes cars are produced in different plants in Germany and around the world.

THE THREE-POINTED STAR

In 1900, an entrepreneur named Emil Jellinek joined the Daimler company. That same year, the company started producing cars under the name of Mercedes. The name was chosen in honor of Jellinek's daughter. In 1909, the Daimler company started using a three-pointed star as a logo. The name Mercedes was added to the three-pointed star in 1916.

When Daimler-Benz AG was created in 1926, the name Benz and a laurel wreath were also added to the logo. Today, all Mercedes-Benz **models** sport the three-pointed star surrounded by a silver ring.

The laurel wreath was originally part of the Benz logo.

MERCEDES-BENZ LOGO

The three points of the star symbolize Mercedes-Benz's desire for its engines to be used on land, sea, and air.

The silver color represents elegance, creativity, and perfection.

MERCEDES-BENZ THROUGH HISTORY

Daimler and Benz joined forces to create the Mercedes-Benz brand. Today, Mercedes-Benz is one of the most celebrated luxury car brands in the world.

Bertha Benz drives the Benz Patent Motor Car for 180 miles (290 kilometers). She proves that the car is reliable and works well for daily use.

1888

1900

1926

The Daimler company starts naming some of its cars after Mercedes Jellinek.

Daimler-Benz AG is created. The first cars under the Mercedes-Benz brand arrive on the market.

Daimler-Benz AG merges with the Chrysler Corporation and changes its name to DaimlerChrysler AG. The company's name is changed again to Daimler AG in 2007.

1998

2019

Daimler AG creates a **subsidiary** company called Mercedes-Benz AG. The company is in charge of producing and selling Mercedes-Benz cars and vans.

2021

Mercedes-Benz competes in the **Formula 1 (F1)** season with the Mercedes-AMG F1 W12 E Performance car.

FAMOUS MERCEDES-BENZ CARS

Several well-known movies helped make Mercedes-Benz extremely popular. An AMG Vision Gran Turismo appeared in the superhero movie *Justice League*. Mercedes-Benz vehicles were also featured in some movies in the Jurassic Park franchise.

Over time, Mercedes-Benz has become a **status symbol**, or a way to show elegance and class. Celebrities of the past enjoyed driving Mercedes-Benz vehicles. Legendary movie star Clark Gable owned a 300 SL Roadster. Princess Diana had a 500 SL.

G-Class sport utility vehicles (SUVs) and Sprinter vans appeared in *Jurassic World*, starring actors Chris Pratt and Bryce Dallas Howard.

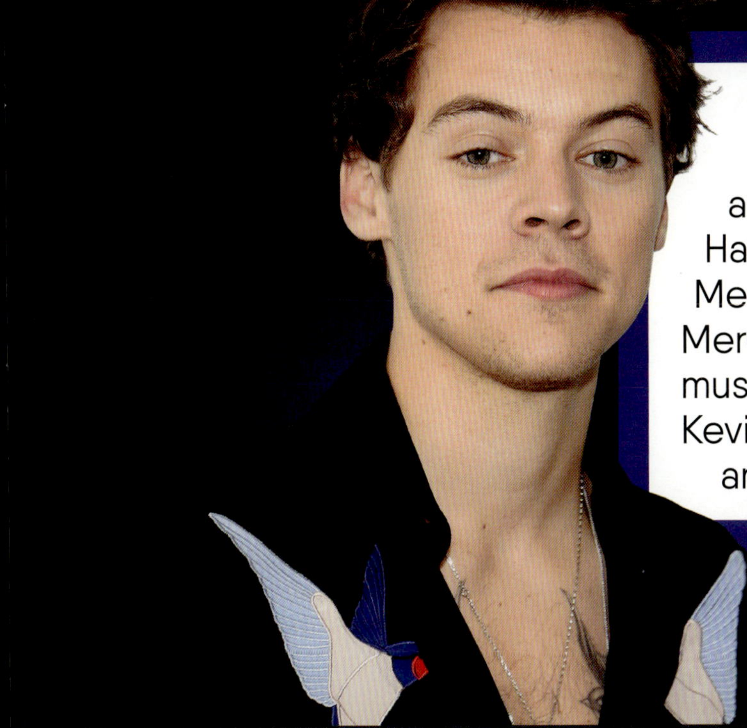

Many modern-day stars are Mercedes lovers as well. Singer and actor Harry Styles owns a vintage Mercedes-Benz. Other Mercedes-Benz fans include music star Drake, comedians Kevin Hart and Rowan Atkinson, and actress Sandra Bullock.

Harry Styles's car collection includes a 1966 Mercedes-Benz 230 SL.

Princess Diana's 500 SL can be seen in the Gallery of Celebrities at the Mercedes-Benz Museum in Stuttgart.

The AMG Vision Gran Turismo was a concept car. Concept cars are built to show off new technologies and designs.

AT THE RACES

Two vehicles with Daimler engines won the first car race in history. This race was held in France in 1894. Daimler-Benz AG's cars continued to race, with some breaks, until 1955. At the end of that year, the company decided to withdraw from sport racing.

Mercedes-Benz vehicles returned to racing in the 1980s. They entered F1 again in 1994. Mercedes-Benz raced together with other car makers until 2009. It then established its own F1 team in 2010. This team was the first to win seven consecutive F1 Constructors' World Championships. They won them between 2014 and 2020.

In 1955, driver Stirling Moss won the Mille Miglia, a 1,000-mile (1,600-km) race, driving a Mercedes-Benz 300 SLR. He completed the race in a record time of 10 hours and 7 minutes.

The first Daimler car to be called Mercedes was a race car, the Mercedes 35 HP.

Only **75** **Mercedes-Benz SLR McLaren Stirling Moss** cars were ever produced.

Lewis Hamilton has been racing with the Mercedes-Benz F1 team since 2013. To date, he has won six F1 Drivers' World Championships with the team.

Lewis Hamilton holds the **record** for the **most race wins in F1**. He has won **99 races** as of July 2020.

Mercedes-Benz honored Stirling Moss in 2009 with the release of the Mercedes-Benz SLR McLaren Stirling Moss roadster.

HOW IT'S MADE

Designers, engineers, and production departments work together to create new Mercedes-Benz cars. Each new vehicle starts as a sketch. Next, different virtual and three-dimensional (3D) models of the sketch are created. They are used to define the look and characteristics of the new vehicle. Then, a life-sized model is built. The model is presented to the Mercedes-Benz board. If the model is successful, the new vehicle can finally move into production. Approved vehicles are built in many different plants and production sites in 17 countries around the world.

One of the oldest Mercedes-Benz plants is in Sindelfingen, near Stuttgart. It was founded in 1915.

The plant in Tuscaloosa, Alabama, was the first Mercedes-Benz major production plant outside Germany. It opened in 1995.

The Mercedes-Benz plant in **Tuscaloosa**, Alabama, has more than **4,000 employees**.

In 2020, a new state-of-the-art plant called Factory 56 opened in Sindelfingen. Mercedes-Benz plans to upgrade all of its plants following this plant's example.

Factory 56 has an area of about **2.4 million square feet** (220,000 square meters).

It can take years for new Mercedes-Benz cars to move from the sketch stage into production.

TODAY'S LINEUP

Mercedes-Benz makes a wide range of vehicles. The brand's current lineup includes elegant SUVs, **sedans**, wagons, and other types of cars. Mercedes-Benz also manufactures vans and trucks.

Here are some of the Mercedes-Benz vehicles on the road today.

Mercedes-Benz GLE 450 4matic SUV

Engine: **3.0L inline-6 turbo with EQ Boost**

Maximum Horsepower: **362**

0–60 mph (0–100 km/h): **5.5 seconds**

Starting Price: **$62,500**

Mercedes-Benz CLS 450 Coupe

Engine: **3.0L inline-6 turbo with EQ Boost**

Maximum Horsepower: **362**

0–60 mph (0–100 km/h): **5.1 seconds**

Starting Price: **$70,300**

Mercedes-Benz AMG C 63 S Cabriolet

Engine: **AMG 4.0L V8 Biturbo**

Maximum Horsepower: **503**

0–60 mph (0–100 km/h): **3.9 seconds**

Starting Price: **$85,600**

Mercedes-Benz AMG E 63 S Wagon

Engine: **AMG 4.0L V8 Biturbo**

Maximum Horsepower: **603**

0–60 mph (0–100 km/h): **3.4 seconds**

Starting Price: **$112,450**

Mercedes-Benz AMG G 63 SUV

Engine: **AMG 4.0L V8 Biturbo**

Maximum Horsepower: **577**

0–60 mph (0–100 km/h): **4.5 seconds**

Starting Price: **$156,450**

Mercedes-Benz AMG GT C Roadster

Engine: **4.0L AMG V8 Biturbo**

Maximum Horsepower: **550**

0–60 mph (0–100 km/h): **3.6 seconds**

Starting Price: **$165,100**

TOMORROW'S MERCEDES-BENZ

Mercedes-Benz plans will focus on protecting the environment in coming years. The company aims to have more than 50 percent of its total sales from **hybrid** or electric vehicles by 2030. By 2022, 10 new electric vehicles, part of the Mercedes-Benz EQ series, will arrive on the market.

In 2020, Mercedes-Benz presented one of its most futuristic concept cars, the VISION AVTR. This concept car was inspired by the popular movie *Avatar*. Devices similar to scales on the back of the VISION AVTR allow drivers to communicate with the outside of the vehicle. The car can move sideways. It is powered by four electric motors and can travel for more than 435 miles (700 km) with one charge. Its battery can be fully charged in less than 15 minutes.

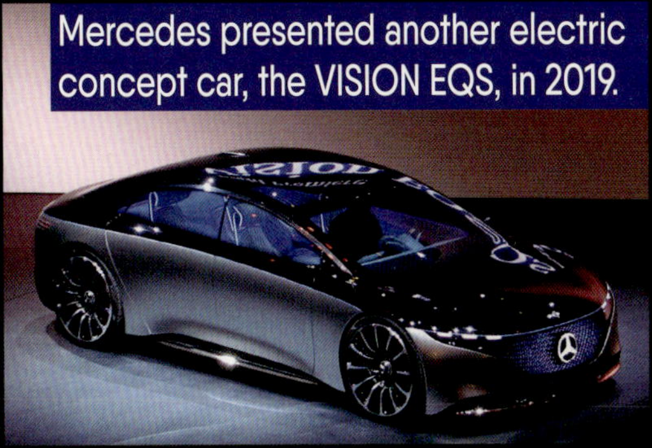

Mercedes presented another electric concept car, the VISION EQS, in 2019.

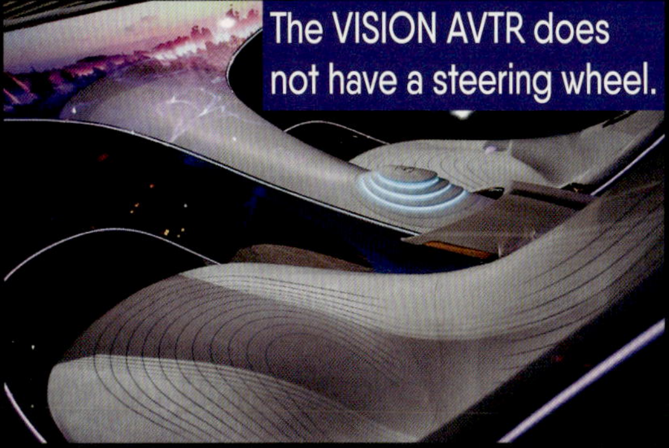

The VISION AVTR does not have a steering wheel.

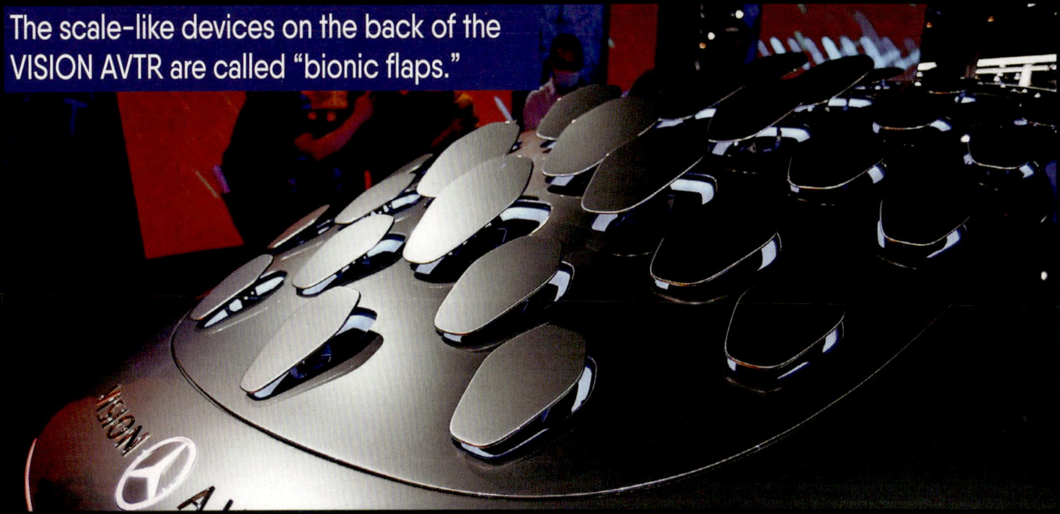

The scale-like devices on the back of the VISION AVTR are called "bionic flaps."

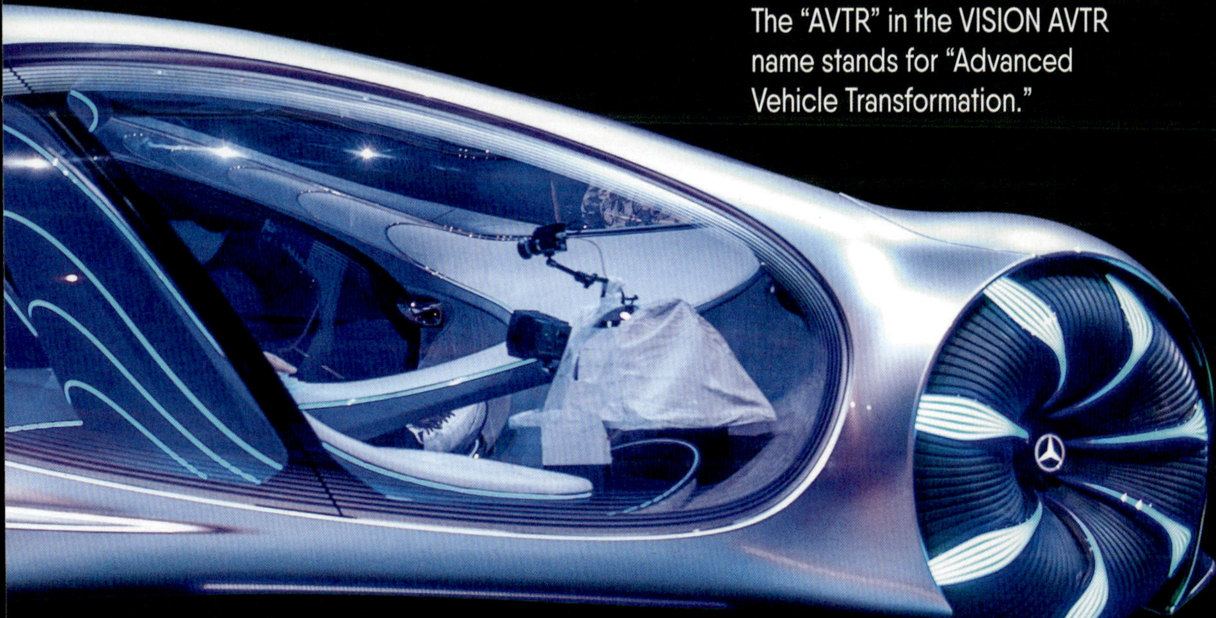

The "AVTR" in the VISION AVTR name stands for "Advanced Vehicle Transformation."

MERCEDES-BENZ QUIZ

1 What does "AVTR" in the VISION AVTR name stand for?

2 When was Factory 56 opened?

3 Which Mercedes-Benz car does Harry Styles own?

4 When was Daimler-Benz AG created?

5 Which Mercedes-Benz car appeared in the movie *Justice League*?

6 Where are the Mercedes-Benz Headquarters?

7 How long does it take for the VISION AVTR's battery to fully charge?

8 Where was the first Mercedes-Benz major production plant outside Germany built?

9 When was the VISION EQS concept car presented?

10 What did Carl Benz patent in 1886?

ANSWERS

1 "Advanced Vehicle Transformation" **2** In 2020 **3** A 1966 Mercedes-Benz 230 SL **4** 1926 **5** An AMG Vision Gran Turismo **6** In Stuttgart, Germany **7** 15 minutes **8** Tuscaloosa, Alabama **9** 2019 **10** A vehicle powered by a gasoline engine

KEY WORDS

engineers: people trained in how to build things and use different materials

exclusive: limited in number

Formula 1 (F1): the highest level of single-seat car racing

hybrid: a car that is powered by both a gas engine and an electric motor

luxurious: something that is pleasing, comfortable, and expensive

merged: united to create one company

models: the different car designs made by a company

patented: obtained the right to exclusively make and sell an invention

sedans: cars that sit four or more people and have roofs that are fixed in place

stagecoach: a covered vehicle usually pulled by horses

status symbol: something that shows wealth and high status

subsidiary: a company that belongs to another company

INDEX

Published by Lightbox Learning
276 5th Avenue, Suite 704 #917
New York, NY 10001
Website: www.openlightbox.com

Library of Congress Cataloging-in-Publication Data

Names: Webster, Christine, author.
Title: Mercedes-Benz / Christine Webster.
Description: New York, NY : AV2, [2022] | Series: Supercars | Includes index. | Audience: Grades 2-3.
Identifiers: LCCN 2021022199 (print) | LCCN 2021022200 (ebook) | ISBN 9781791138875 (library binding) | ISBN 9781791138882 (paperback) | ISBN 9781791138899 (ebook other)
Subjects: LCSH: Mercedes automobiles--Juvenile literature. | Sports car racing--Juvenile literature.
Classification: LCC TL215.M4 W43 2022 (print) | LCC TL215.M4 (ebook) | DDC 629.222/2--dc23
LC record available at https://lccn.loc.gov/2021022199
LC ebook record available at https://lccn.loc.gov/2021022200

Printed in Guangzhou, China
1 2 3 4 5 6 7 8 9 0 25 24 23 22 21

072021
101120

Art Director: Terry Paulhus
Project Coordinator: Sara Cucini

Photo Credits
Every reasonable effort has been made to trace ownership and to obtain permission to reprint copyright material. The publisher would be pleased to have any errors or omissions brought to its attention so that they may be corrected in subsequent printings. The publisher acknowledges Getty Images, Alamy, Shutterstock, and Dreamstime as its primary image suppliers for this title.